WE'VE GOT CHARACTER!

I TAKE TURNS

BY CHARLOTTE TAYLOR

Gareth Stevens
PUBLISHING

Please visit our website, www.garethstevens.com. For a free color catalog of all our high-quality books, call toll free 1-800-542-2595 or fax 1-877-542-2596.

Library of Congress Cataloging-in-Publication Data

Names: Taylor, Charlotte, author.
Title: I take turns / Charlotte Taylor.
Description: New York : Gareth Stevens Publishing, 2021. | Series: We've got character! | Includes bibliographical references and index.
Identifiers: LCCN 2019047950 | ISBN 9781538256299 (library binding) | ISBN 9781538256275 (paperback) | ISBN 9781538256282 (6 Pack) | ISBN 9781538256305 (ebook)
Subjects: LCSH: Patience–Juvenile literature.
Classification: LCC BJ1533.P3 T39 2020 | DDC 179/.9–dc23
LC record available at https://lccn.loc.gov/2019047950

Published in 2021 by
Gareth Stevens Publishing
111 East 14th Street, Suite 349
New York, NY 10003

Designer: Sarah Liddell
Editor: Megan Quick

Photo credits: Cover, p. 1 Monkey Business Images/Shutterstock.com; background throughout Igor Vitkovskiy/Shutterstock.com; p. 5 Karen Struthers/Shutterstock.com; p. 7 monkeybusinessimages/iStock/Getty Images Plus/Getty Images; p. 9 Hispanolistic/E+/Getty Images; p. 11 Juanmonino/E+/Getty Images; p. 13 gpointstudio/Shutterstock.com; p. 15 sirtravelalot/Shutterstock.com; p. 17 Happy Together/Shutterstock.com; p. 19 CREATISTA/Shutterstock.com; p. 21 yacobchuk/iStock/Getty Images Plus/Getty Images.

CPSIA compliance information: Batch #CS20GS: For further information contact Gareth Stevens, New York, New York at 1-800-542-2595.

Find us on

CONTENTS

Boldface words appear in the glossary.

Why Do We Take Turns?

Sometimes many people want to do the same thing. But only one person can do it at a time. You may have to be **patient** and wait for your turn. Taking turns gives everyone a chance. Taking turns is fair.

Wait for It

Anna was eating dinner with her family. She wanted to tell them about a movie she saw at school that day. But Anna's brother was talking about his day. Anna listened to her brother. She waited until it was her turn to talk.

Julio went shopping for food with his mom. When it was time to pay, there was a long line of people ahead of them. Julio and his mom had to wait for their turn to pay. They had to be patient.

9

Share the Work

Every week, Sarah and her sister had to take out the **garbage**. They took turns doing the job. One week, Sarah took out the garbage. The next week, her sister did. Sometimes taking turns makes a job easier for everyone.

Share the Fun

Will and his friends went to the park. Everyone wanted to go on the slide. They did not push and **shove**. They got in a line. They took turns going down the slide. When friends take turns, everyone can have fun!

Kate and her brother got a new **video game**. They both wanted to try it. They decided to take turns. Kate played the game for 30 minutes. Then she let her brother play for the same amount of time. They shared the game by taking turns.

Helen's class got a new pet bunny! Everyone wanted to take it home for the weekend. The teacher made a list with each child's name on it. She **assigned** everyone a weekend. They all took turns bringing home the bunny.

Let's Talk

Finn was new in town. Joe walked to school with him. Joe asked Finn about his **favorite** sport. Finn said he liked soccer. Then he asked Joe what sports he liked. They took turns listening and speaking. They had a good **conversation**.

Tanya's class was working in small groups. Each person in her group shared their ideas. The others listened. They did not **interrupt**. Tanya talked when it was her turn. Her group worked well together because they took turns talking.

GLOSSARY

assign: to give out a specific job or task

conversation: a talk between two or more people

favorite: liked best

garbage: waste or trash

interrupt: to begin to talk when another person is talking

patient: able to wait a long time

shove: to push hard

video game: an electronic game that involves players controlling characters on a TV or computer screen

FOR MORE INFORMATION

BOOKS

Rankin, Laura. *My Turn!* New York, NY: Bloomsbury, 2016.

Miller, Pat Zietlow. *Be Kind.* New York, NY: Roaring Brook Press, 2018.

WEBSITES

Life's Little Lessons: Sharing
pbskids.org/learn/lifes-little-lessons/sharing/
Watch a fun video about sharing and taking turns.

How to Teach Your Child to Take Turns
cainclusion.org/resources/tp/materials/backpack-series/bkpk_turns.pdf
Find ideas for how to practice taking turns.

INDEX